DATE DUE

Tough Topics

Moving

Patricia J. Murphy

Heinemann Library
Chicago, Illinois

Customer Service   888–454–2279

Visit our Web site at www.heinemannlibrary.com

Photo research by Erica Martin
Designed by Richard Parker and Q2A Creative
Printed and bound in China by South China Printing Company

09 08 07
10 9 8 7 6 5 4 3 2 1

Library of Congress Cataloging-in-Publication Data
Murphy, Patricia J., 1963–
 Moving / Patricia J. Murphy.
 p.cm. – (Tough Topics)
 Includes index
 ISBN 978-1-4034-9776-5 (hardback)   ISBN 978-1-4034-9781-9 (pbk)
 1. Moving, Household-Juvenile literature. 2. Moving, Household-Psychological aspects-Juvenile literature. I. Title
 TX307.M875 2007
 684'.9–dc22
                2007005346

Acknowledgments
The publishers would like to thank the following for permission to reproduce photographs:
© Corbis pp. **6** (Zave Smith), **22** (Tim Pannell), **5**; © Getty Images pp. **11** (Taxi/Arthur Tilley), **12** (The Image Bank/Brooklyn Productions), **15** (Peter Dazeley), **17** (Photodisc), **19** (Gary Houlder), **23** (The Image Bank/Florian Franke), **29** (Digital Vision); © Masterfile pp. **4** (Michael Mahovlich), **8** (Jerzyworks), **9** (David Schmidt); © Photoedit pp. **7**, **13** (David Young-Wolff), **20** (Michael Newman); © Photolibrary p. **26** (Purestock), **28** (Veer Incorporated - Fancy); © Photolibrary.com p. **21**; © Punchstock pp. **10** (Chris Carroll), **18** (Uppercut Images/Robert Houser), **24** (Uppercut Images/Hill Creek Pictures), **25** (UpperCut Images), **16**, **27**; © Superstock p. **14** (Stockdisc)

Cover photograph of for sale sign reproduced with permission of © Corbis/image100.

Every effort has been made to contact copyright holders of any material reproduced in this book. Any omissions will be rectified in subsequent printings if notice is given to the publisher.

Contents

Some words are shown in bold, **like this**. You can find out what they mean by looking in the Glossary.

Moving

Things are always moving. Birds fly south for the winter. Other animals also **migrate**, going to a new home as the seasons change. People also move from place to place.

Some people move many times in their lives. Each move brings new experiences—some happy and some difficult.

Why Do People Move?

▲ Families often need a bigger home when new children are born.

People move for different reasons. Someone in the family may have a new job in a different place. Some people may wish to buy bigger or smaller homes. Others may want to live closer to loved ones.

Other people might choose to move to a warmer **climate** or to see other parts of the world. Whatever the reason, moving can be hard because you leave behind special people and places.

▶ Leaving people you love behind is hard.

How Do People Move?

Some people move far away from their old home. Some move just a few blocks. Either way, you must take everything with you when you move.

Before moving, you have to pack all of your things into boxes. Next, you need to load these boxes into cars or large trucks. Some people use a moving company to help them move.

Getting Ready to Move

◄ You might worry how you will feel in your new surroundings.

Moving can be exciting, but it can also be scary. You may wonder if you will like your new town, new home, and new school.

You can look up information on your new town at the library or on the **Internet**. You could also visit before you move and meet some people who live there.

▲ Talking about your new home with your family will help you get ready to move.

Saying Goodbye

Before moving away, you may want to say goodbye to family members, friends, and familiar places in your **neighborhood**. Your family may have a party to say goodbye.

▶It is hard to leave a special place behind.

You might also say goodbye to your home. You could walk from room to room and remember the good times that you had in them. You can take these **memories** with you when you leave.

Staying in Touch

When people move, they usually give their new address and phone number to family and friends before they leave. They may also take pictures to remember them.

▲ A photo of your friends will help you feel better if you miss them.

It is important to stay in touch with
friends and family after you move. Phone
calls, letters, emails, and visits will help
you stay in touch. This might make
moving away less sad for everyone.

Moving Day

Moving day is a busy day. Boxes and furniture are moved out of the old home and into the new one. It can take days or weeks to unpack and get everything into the right place.

▲ Moving heavy furniture is hard work.

▲ Unpacking can be fun if you do it together.

Moving can be exciting, but it is also tiring and **stressful**. People may argue and get upset more easily on moving day. It is normal for these things to happen.

How Does It Feel to Move?

Some children may be happy to move. They might see moving as a new adventure. They may be excited about living in a new place, **neighborhood**, and **community**.

▶ It can be fun to get out and explore your new neighborhood.

Many people might be sad or angry about moving away from family and friends. They may also be afraid they might not fit in or make new friends. Sometimes, people have a mix of these feelings.

Moving In

When you arrive at your new home, everything you loaded into the cars and moving van has to be moved in. Then you have to unpack the boxes. Things will be all over the place!

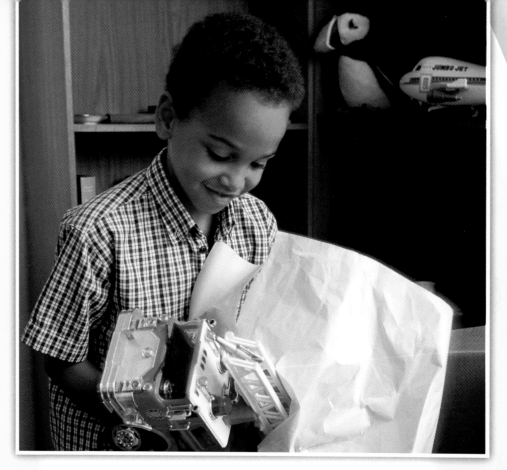

▲ It can be fun to unpack your favorite things.

Unpacking can be a happy time when you find places to put your things. It can also be upsetting when you cannot find things that you need. While you pack, it is a good idea to label your boxes so you know what is inside of them.

New Places

▲ Get a map of your new town to help you find your way around.

A new town has many new places to discover. These places may include new stores, parks, schools, libraries, museums, and **community** centers.

To find these places, you could walk or ride around town with an adult. You could stop by the town's **city hall**, **chamber of commerce**, or **visitors' center** to ask questions or directions.

▲ Introduce yourself to neighbors and other people you meet.

Loneliness

Being in a new town can be **lonely**. Neighbors are strangers at first, and family and friends may feel far away. You may wonder when you will start to fit in.

▲ It is normal to miss the people and places you have left behind.

▲ If you feel lonely for a long time,
share your feelings with a parent
or trusted adult.

With a little time and effort, you will feel
like a part of your new town and meet
new friends. Try to look for good things
in your new home and neighborhood.

Making New Friends

Making new friends is not always easy. Sometimes it takes hard work. Some people might not seem very friendly. Others might act like they do not need any new friends.

◄ It can be hard to tell if someone wants to be your friend.

▶ Playing a sport is a great way to meet people.

To make friends, you have to be brave. You have to say hello and tell people your name. You could join a club or sign up for a team sport. Some of the people you meet might turn into friends.

Feeling at Home

Once you have unpacked all the boxes and put things away, you will begin to feel comfortable in your new home. Soon your sad feelings will go away.

▲ It is normal to have sad feelings about moving.

▲ Family is what makes any place feel like home.

For most people, moving is a good experience. It teaches you how to handle change. Often times, it can bring families closer together.

Moving Tips

- Label all of your boxes with a marker. For example, label boxes for your clothes, books, and awards. This will make it easier to find things when you unpack.

- Pack a moving day bag. Put things like your toothbrush and favorite book in this bag and keep it with you on moving day. This way, you will have what you need before you are completely unpacked.

- Set up your room the way you want it as soon as you can. This will help you feel more at home.

- Take your time unpacking. Do not try to do it all at once. Take some breaks and spend time with your family. Your things will be there when you get back.

- Visit the town with your family and introduce yourself to your neighbors. Soon, your new town will feel like home.

Glossary

city hall where the city's government offices are located

chamber of commerce group of businesses (stores, restaurants, services) that works to improve a town's community

climate usual weather in a region or area

Internet computer network that links computers worldwide

lonely feeling alone

memories things you remember from your past

migrate change location seasonally from one area to another

neighborhood area in a city or town where people live

stressful causing worry

visitor center place where visitors go to learn more about a city or town

More Books to Read

Davis, Gabriel. *The Moving Book: A Kids' Survival Guide*. Portland, OR: First Books, 2003.

Helmer, Diana. *Let's Talk About Moving to a New Place*. New York: Powerkids Press, 1999.

Maisner, Heather. *We're Moving*. Boston: Kingfisher, 2004.

Mundy, Michaelene. *Saying Goodbye, Saying Hello—When Your Family Is Moving*. St. Meinrad, IN: One Caring Place/Abbey Press, 2005.

Index